All people
have from birth
the same basic needs,
there are at least 12

The contents of this book
can be a valuable contribution
to the development of a much more
humane future.

Publisher: BoD · Books on Demand GmbH
In de Tarpen 42, 22848 Norderstedt
Print: Libri Plureos GmbH, Friedensalle 273,
22763 Hamburg, www.bod.de
ISBN: 978-3-7693-2172-2

First version in German 2022

The little basic needs book

A walkable path

von

Michael Johanni
Human rights activist

2022 / 2024

Humanity makes the difference

Being human

You were born human.
Therefore - live humanly, think humanly, decide humanly, because this is the way for all of us.

Prologue

The day is coming when we will stand before the wide-open gates of a world in which the top priority will always be to promote and protect humanity in all areas of life.

We are still a long way from this - as evidenced by the strong fears that the majority of us citizens carry with us on an almost daily basis.

Oppressive poverty and painful homelessness also show that 'people' have placed themselves above us, for whom a livable existence is a thorn in the side of the population.

That is why, in our own interest, we must reflect on the natural strengths that we all carry within us from birth.

We should form a real community!

Such a community is created as soon as we support each other, complement each other regularly and respect the basic needs of all citizens.

My vision

A truly balanced social structure will have a positive impact and lead to a much more humane global community that is supplied with all the necessary goods.

Freedom

Freedom arises from justice.

Justice arises on the basis of truth.

You find **truth** where true humanity comes first - and that is where freedom manifests itself.

The difference between a need and a basic need

A need can be arbitrary - for example, wanting the latest smartphone, the latest TV or a faster car.

Our basic needs, on the other hand, are not arbitrary - we carry them within us from birth.
They form an essential part of our natural human characteristics and therefore influence our existence.
Everything we do and experience is directly related to them.

THE CIRCLE OF BASIC NEEDS

by Michael Johanni 2015
Human rights activist and author

A ‘key’

One of the keys to a much more humane world lies in the conscious, mutual consideration of our basic needs.

12 basic needs

food

Sleep

Basic need to communicate
The natural desire to communicate

Curiosity

Security
In all areas of life

Affection
In all areas of life

Recognition
In all areas of life

Harmony
In all areas of life

Reproduction
The natural desire to preserve the human species.

Sexuality

Freedom of expression
The natural desire to exprcss a useful opinion

Creativity The natural
desire for mental stimulation, to acquire skills, to live and expand them

It is our natural right

We humans have the natural right to approach happiness.

The basic need
Food

We humans need a balanced diet.
Depending on your physical tolerance, eat at least one portion of fruit and vegetables a day. Vegetables should only be gently cooked, not boiled.
Nutrients such as vitamins (preferably of natural origin), fibre and minerals as well as monounsaturated and polyunsaturated fatty acids, such as omega-3 and omega-6 fatty acids, for example from high-quality linseed and olive oil, walnuts and avocado, are very beneficial for our health.
A low consumption of meat and sausages is also good for our health. Readymade products should be removed from the diet.
Avoid sugar and sugary drinks as much as possible. Chemical sweeteners are harmful to our health! It is also important to ensure that we drink enough fluids every day - 2.5 to approx. 3 litres. In the evening, it is advisable not to eat anything or only very light food for about three hours before going to bed.

Be authentic

We humans are born friendly beings, we don't have to force ourselves to be.
We should only trust ourselves to be humanly authentic, then many things will come naturally.

The basic need
Sleep

The human biological structure encompasses body and mind in equal measure. Because this is the case, sufficient, relaxed sleep means an immense amount - the latter applies above all to strengthening our immune system.

Working at night makes us age and fall ill more quickly. That is why we should only work late in the evening and at night where it is really necessary - e.g. in hospices, palliative care units, nursing homes, hospitals, rescue services, fire brigades, bus, train and taxi companies.

Let us always pay attention to our biological rhythm, which is closely linked to the times of day and night.

The place in the heart

Your true home is not a house, a flat or a place, but the place in the hearts of understanding family members, real friends and other people who care about you.

The need to communicate
basic need

It is completely in line with human nature to want to communicate with other people.
If we do not communicate with each other - through language, gestures and facial expressions - we are stuck in limitation, isolation and loneliness.
Many trains of thought lose their meaning because they are not passed on to fellow citizens.

We are in the right environment,
as soon as it gives us pleasure,
with other people about almost anything.

‘You have to be able to see

be able to see the way

saw the world as a child.’

Henri Matisse 1869-1954
Painter, graphic artist
sculptor

The basic need
Curiosity

Our curiosity is a wonderful thing - a truly valuable gift of nature.
Being able to be curious means living in an environment in which interpersonal openness is valued as a natural part of positive interaction.

Without natural curiosity, we humans remain within a narrow circle of thought, so that our horizons barely extend beyond the edge of our plate.

Therefore - live - be curious and use the knowledge for an existence in dignity and for a truly human community.

Privacy

Every citizen
must have the human right
to a dignified home so that their
privacy has sufficient space
and protection.

The basic need
Security

Security is the warm blanket that each of us needs.

Feeling safe and secure means being able to let go. To know that you are here and now in an environment that is imbued with sincere trust.
It's like having a warm blanket gently placed over your freezing body.
Feeling at home because there are people here who care about you - who have nothing else in mind but your well-being.

Truth

‘Truth often doesn't need
many words,
sometimes none at all.’

Christine Werth
Human rights activist

The basic need
Affection

Affection is

the sincere attention

that we give our fellow human beings

to our fellow human beings.

Each of us needs the sincere word and empathy of our fellow human beings - in a wide variety of situations.

Affection makes us feel that we belong and are accepted, that we are not marginalised.
We need the hand that takes ours - especially when disappointment, loneliness and illness cloud the joy of life.

‘We tend to judge success by the size of our salaries or the size of our cars - but not by the degree of our helpfulness and the measure of our humanity.’

Martin Luther King Jr. 1929-1968
Human rights activist
Nobel Peace Prize winner

The basic need *Recognition*

The treasure of recognition is everywhere,

We should waste it.

The inner desire for recognition is of universal importance - it is all-encompassing, particularly far-reaching and affects all thoughts and actions with deep sustainability.

Recognition is important for us humans in all areas of life.

Even a favourable glance, a sincere thank you and noticing and expressing appreciation even for 'small' changes/improvements boost motivation in everyone.

Truth creates peace

From the moment when the truth becomes more important to many citizens than privileges, prestige status and fears, the world will change significantly in the interests of humanity.

The basic need
Harmony

As soon as we listen to ourselves more consciously, we hear the longing for harmony - this is by no means a sentimental desire.
It is much more about the very natural basic need to be in harmony with our fellow human beings, our environment and ourselves.

It is important that we allow ourselves to strive for harmony.
We can only achieve a truly balanced existence if we build harmonious relationships with our fellow human beings.
Making an effort to understand others is a worthwhile step towards empathy.

The naturalness of life

If we humans do not
correspond to nature,
it overtakes us before we
even realise its gift - life.

The basic need *Reproduction*

The inner desire to reproduce is a close ally of the subconscious and the instinct for self-preservation.
Together, these three notable characte-ristics are fundamentally concerned first and foremost with ensuring the survival of us humans.
At the same time, this is linked to the intuitive but concrete idea of a conti-nuation of life after death, in that we hold on to the justified hope that a part of our ego, a part of our thoughts, will at best continue to exist in other people.

Reproduction - the natural desire, to preserve the human species.

First and foremost

In all areas of life
and in all decisions,
people and their basic needs
must come first.

The basic need *Sexuality*

Our daily existence is more strongly influenced by the natural desire for sexuality than we often realise.
We humans are made up of body, mind and emotions - as soon as we can live this amazing connection holistically, we feel completely at ease. Happiness becomes tangible.

Nevertheless, we need to use our common sense.
With regard to the health and dignity of our fellow human beings, including ourselves, we must never allow ourselves to be carried away by pursuing sexual desire 'at any price'.
In a harmonious partner relationship, there are plenty of ways to give sexuality the attention it deserves.

Expression of opinion and truth

The actual right to freedom of expression only exists when the search for the truth and the publication of facts that serve to establish the truth do not lead to the marginalisation or punishment of those who seek the truth.

The basic need
Freedom of expression

It is undoubtedly a special characteristic of our nature to have the desire to express a useful opinion.

After all, our mental disposition is naturally created to conceptualise processes, to form words in order to categorise them linguistically.

From this, the natural urge to express oneself develops all by itself.

Expressing one's personal views is very important for everyone. By exchanging opinions and arguments, we can make the most sense of a situation.

Our statements should always be accompanied by the claim to truth and the search for truth.

The first steps

If you want to make a serious contribution to a much more humane society, one of your first steps should be to stop clinging to all the usual routines.

The basic need
Creativity

Creativity is the natural desire for mental encouragement to acquire, live and expand skills.

We need a favourable environment in order to be able to develop our creativity.
If we are deprived of such an environment, this special source gradually dries up within us.
It is therefore very important to always ensure that our development potential is not restricted.
We humans have a natural right to free development, especially in spiritual terms.

Development

Where people are trimmed for performance from an early age, the development of their natural qualities falls by the wayside.
Our mental, emotional and physical development must be guaranteed at all times!

Support system
Dignity

Human dignity is an important, natural part of our ego.
It is a superordinate, firmly anchored, permanent process of consciousness that is constantly given tangible, existential substance through the elementary basic needs and their human-specific desire.
Our dignity thus becomes a mental, emotional 'support structure' that forms the basis for all thought processes and behaviour.

We need warmth

Every human soul needs a warming scarf so that moral coldness and resentment can cause it as little damage as possible.

What luck

As soon as we truly and completely realise how lucky we are to live on this earth, the path to a natural, meaningful journey of existence is revealed to us.

A little about me

Hardly a day goes by when I am not deeply touched by what has been happening on this earth for a long time.
It is therefore understandable that I have an incorrigible desire for harmony and peace among us humans.

I was born on 4 December 1962 in Schweinfurt/Northern Bavaria.
I came to my present level of knowledge because I recognised and used my autodidactic abilities. This has enabled me to question and conscientiously analyse the natural, life-determining basic needs (at least 12), their existential significance and important socio-political contexts much more consciously for over 20 years.
In addition, I have had countless conversations with citizens in various places, and I continue to do so.
I began writing down my extensive analyses and findings in 2001, and in 2008 I founded the association ...mensch bleib Mensch!

If you would like to tell me something about the contents of my books and other topics, please use the following addresses:

mail@michael-johanni.de
www.michael-johanni.de
www.buecher-charakter.de
www.mensch-bleib-mensch.de

Michael Johanni
Human rights activist,
founder and author

My other works

Dear reader,
It is my wish to gradually translate more books into English.

Ein Meer aus bewegten Gedanken für eine Welt in Frieden

Erlesenes Nachschlagewerk mit 400 bedeutsamen Aphorismen & Kurztexten verfasst 2005-2024

***Hardcover,** 180 Seiten, ISBN: 978-3-7597-0241-8*

Das Gute wird sich durchsetzen

Unser menschliches Potential
Hindernisse und Chancen

152 Seiten, ISBN: 978-3-7578-2487-7

Raus aus der Apathie

Welcher Wert liegt im Leiden?

276 Seiten, ISBN: 978-3-7543-9739-8

Lila Bäume

Sobald wir genauer hinsehen ...

152 Seiten, ISBN: 978-3-7557-4150-3

Please continue on the next page

... damit das Morgen eine Aussicht hat

Zwei Eingänge

60 Seiten, ISBN: 978-3-7557-7986-5

Zukunft braucht Courage

Abwarten bringt uns nicht weiter!

256 Seiten, ISBN: 978-3-7568-8786-6

Verwandle deine Hoffnung in Ziele

Motivierende Aphorismen & Kurztexte

80 Seiten, ISBN: 978-3-7583-7363-3

Ich glaube, die Blätter sprechen miteinander

Meine Gedanken

Kurztexte

60 Seiten, ISBN: 978-3-7578-0325-4

... verschüttet, aber nicht verloren

Du hast mindestens 12 Grundbedürfnisse

Kurztexte

80 Seiten, ISBN: 978-3-7557-1509-2

My previous books are published by
BoD-Books on Demand GmbH, Norderstedt,
Germany.

The journey of life

Neither in power nor in money,
the true meaning of human existence is
found in a sincere, dignified journey
through life.

www.ingramcontent.com/pod-product-compliance
Lightning Source LLC
LaVergne TN
LVHW042237190726

843491LV00003BA/1102
* 9 7 8 3 7 6 9 3 2 1 7 2 2 *